The Baseball Success Handbook

15 Secrets Every Player Needs, starting with Little League, to Rise to Big League

Every year, Major League Baseball and other professional leagues look to draft new recruits for their organizations. They are looking for players who will elevate their game. Every season, players get released from professional baseball for poor, inconsistent performance.

In this revolutionary Itty Bitty® Baseball Handbook, Curt and Amy give you the secrets that set major league champions apart.

Is Your Dream to Play in the Big League?

Following these 15 powerful secrets will help you reach your dreams. Faster than you think:

- Develop the mental game required in handling disappointment and pursuing your passion.
- Create habits that are simple to execute and easy to integrate into existing practice routines.
- Develop and master self-care habits.
- Cultivate a team of mentors who will give you the edge to get noticed.

Go ahead, open it and start reading Secret 1. Right now! ***Your dreams are closer than you think.***

"I really enjoyed reading this book. Brought me back to the way I used to think when I was playing."
                          -Brian Hunter, MLB player 1991-2000

"Amy and Curt have captured the attitude and work ethics necessary for athletic transformation and placed them in one short book. This book is packed with ingredients and steps to make you a champion in the classroom and on the field. Whether you are a coach, parent or the athlete, this book will change the way you perform in your position. So many of today's super athletes have used the truths in this book to reach and maintain peak performance in their field. As an ex-major leaguer and currently private coach, I am amazed that the secrets inside this book are not being utilized more by today's young athletes. It is a must read for the athlete in you."
                          -Dennis Powell, MLB player 1983-1995

Your Amazing
Itty Bitty®
Baseball Success Book

15 Secrets to Rise from Little League to Big League

Amy Jean - Curt Christiansen

Published by Itty Bitty® Publishing
A subsidiary of S & P Productions, Inc.

Copyright © 2016 Amy Jean-Curt Christiansen

All rights reserved. No part of this book may be reproduced or transmitted in any form or by any means, electronic or mechanical, including photocopying, recording or by any information storage and retrieval system, without written permission of the publisher, except for inclusion of brief quotations in a review.

Printed in the United States of America

Itty Bitty® Publishing
311 Main Street, Suite D
El Segundo, CA 90245
(310) 640-8885
www.ittybittypublishing.com

ISBN: 9781931191630

DEDICATION

This is dedicated to Valerie Gin (When Girls Become Lions) for your inexhaustible pursuit of God's purpose through sport.

To Bryan Hunter and Dennis Powell for sharing your secrets with us and working alongside us to develop future champions, and really take our game to the next level.

To Chris Powell, Andrew Toles, and Kevin Grendell for letting us play a small part as you live your dream.

You realize that secrets learned in Sport are really the lessons of Life. You've been coach, player, mentor and friend. You have touched our lives every time we meet.

Please visit our Itty Bitty Publishing website to learn more about Baseball Success.

www.Ittybittypublishing.com

Want to achieve more? Connect with Curt and Amy and discover the "The Right Approach to Baseball Success" at:

www.TRABaseball.com

Ready to live your dream? So often high schoolers with Big League dreams make **The Biggest Mistake**. They fail to follow a successful plan. The coaches at The Right Approach Baseball Academy have developed The Right Approach Game Plan based on their experiences as they achieved their dreams. We offer this Game Plan as our gift to you. Now is the time to rise.

Access this FREE Game Plan at:

www.TRABaseball.com/GamePlan

Table of Contents

Secret 1.	**P**lay Early, Play Often, Play for FUN
Secret 2.	**E**rrors are *NOT* Failures
Secret 3.	**A**ttitude: Passion and Peak Performance
Secret 4.	**K**eep Your Team Close
Secret 5.	**P**ractice Like It's Game Day
Secret 6.	**E**xpect Success
Secret 7.	**R**emember Where You Started
Secret 8.	**F**ind Your ZONE
Secret 9.	**O**ff the Field and *IN* the Classroom
Secret 10.	**R**egret Nothing
Secret 11.	**M**illion Dollar Asset
Secret 12.	**A**lign Your Mind
Secret 13.	**N**utrition: Junk In, Junk *OUT*
Secret 14.	**C**ompetitive Edge
Secret 15.	**E**levate Your Game

INTRODUCTION

The journey to achieving your dreams isn't easy. Many give up on themselves and their dream before they even start, because they don't have a game plan and lack focused motivation. Many will make knucklehead choices that limit their opportunities before they get their big chance. Or they'll allow fear and self-doubt to sabotage their efforts.

We have worked with coaches and players who have gone before you. Coaches who learned the secrets to live their dreams. Because of our many years of coaching and mentoring experience, we decided to write this Itty Bitty® Book to reveal those secrets to you in a simple success handbook to help you on your journey.

In this Itty Bitty® Baseball Book, you will find 15 secrets to discover and unlock the Champion inside of you. Boy or girl, young or old, we all can unleash the Champion inside. With the right guidance and the right focus, when is the time to decide to live your dreams? Now. Let's get to work.

Your 15 Secrets

Secret 1
Play Early, Play Often, Play for FUN

Every time you step on the field, remind yourself of the love you have for this game. Remind yourself of the very first time you picked up your glove and threw the ball. It's this love that will help you as you develop good habits. The right approach takes time and focused practice.

1. **The Most Important Thing:** Play the game with others that love the game as much as you do.
2. Find programs and coaches who love the game as much as you love it and are as interested in your individual success as you are.
3. Good technique is crucial to achieving your best results. So, play for expert coaches who know the physical, mental and emotional skills required to achieve your dreams.
4. When you join a team, go where you'll get a lot of play time. As a big league coach says, "Better to play where you're going to get at-bats, instead of riding the pine."
5. To play at your highest level, baseball camps and clinics give you the opportunity to totally focus on your game, so you can decrease bad habits and improve good habits faster than only playing for a team.

Play Early, Play Often, Play for FUN

- First! Find what it is that you love. Then, figure out how to do that thing you love.
- To be a Champion, you have to be intentional. The scout isn't going to knock on your door if you never pursue the skill necessary to achieve Peak Performance and your next level.
- If you don't spend time practicing the right techniques, you won't develop the right approach needed to reach your dreams.
- The right camps include players and coaches at all levels, so you can model players who have reached your next level.
- Watch and model professional athletes who play your position, so you can elevate your game.
- Know where you're going. The minor league player chooses self-discipline and makes sacrifices because of his love for the game and his vision of the future.
- Play to improve your mental and physical skill, not for a bigger trophy.
- Without the love, there is no game.

Secret 2
Errors are *NOT* Failures

When an athlete makes a mistake, the first thing he does is hang his head. You can almost hear the negative talk he tells himself. Instead, let your errors create a place for you to learn and grow and develop as you pursue your dreams.

1. The truth is everyone makes mistakes, but the Champion learns from his mistakes and is able to turn them into successes.
2. At camp you learn success isn't perfection. Success is taking responsibility for your mistake and correcting your error with the next play, so you can reach your next level.
3. Once, we watched a MiLB player pitch less than his best. He walked from the mound with his head high and determination on his face. In the locker room, he told his team, "It's on me." The next day he came out even stronger and more determined. At no time did he give up on himself or his team.
4. The only real failure is when you give up on yourself and stop giving your best effort.
5. Fear and worry accomplish nothing except to take away from your strengths and your game plan.
6. There is no time to dwell on your mistakes and errors. If you do, you will miss the next lesson.

Errors are *NOT* Failures

- Each setback gives you a chance to reassess your goals and redirect your actions.
- Visualization is the key to turning errors into success.
- **How to Visualize:** Take the time to see and feel yourself executing each part of each skill you perform, and take a mental picture.
- What do you think and feel when you set up to throw? How are you breathing and feeling through the motion of your throw? When your throw makes that "thud" sound right at the target, how do you feel? What do you tell yourself?
- Recreate that mental picture for your bat performance.
- Successful coaches and camp programs will teach simple visual processes for you to use in your practice and game routines.
- Each time you'll improve because instead of spending your time getting down on yourself, you'll be picking yourself up and rising to your next level.
- The Champion knows he needs to follow his game plan, and learn from his errors to rise to the next level.

Secret 3
Attitude: Passion and Peak Performance

Attitude is what separates the ballplayer from the Champion. Be known for your attitude, not your antics. Champions have heart. Show your heart at every opportunity.

1. The Champion continues to perform at his top level, especially when no one else is watching.
2. To be a Champion you must come with heart. A coach can give you all the technique and training to reach success, but you must start with your heart.
3. To show heart, the Champion never walks or sits down during practice. Run to every position, run to get a drink. Every time you move – RUN.
4. Don't cut corners. The Champion knows that a corner cut during a warm-up lap is a missed opportunity to prepare for the game changing moments ahead.
5. You cannot always avoid frustrating circumstances or people, but a vital part of the Champion's solid game plan is choosing his attitudes and actions when he responds.
6. Be humble and able to take constructive feedback.
7. Cultivate a game-winning attitude from your program coaches.

Attitude: Passion and Peak Performance

- A coach, when they are looking to fill their roster, will choose that next-level player based on attitude, and someone who is easy to train as often, if not more than, the player who may just have talent.
- At camp, your coaches help you to cultivate skill, combined with the attitude that coaches are looking for.
- When you play with heart, you're confident in your own ability without being full of yourself or conceited.
- Never Quit, Never Give IN, Never Surrender and Never Die! – in pursuit of your Great Cause.
- Take your Champion's heart with you in every situation, on and off the field.

Secret 4
Keep Your Team Close

In order to rise, the Champion knows that he needs the support and encouragement of his team. The Champion, also, knows that leadership is about setting the example for his team.

1. The Champion recognizes that his team consists of players, coaches, mentors, managers and family.
2. Each team member deserves your respect and friendship.
3. Champions are leaders. And to be a good leader, you must first be a good example.
4. The Champion will step into leadership and cultivate this camaraderie.
5. To be a Champion, you must be a good teammate.
6. At camp, you learn to support, encourage and uplift the players around you.
7. Decide to like every member of your team.
8. Use your teammates and opponents in your position to motivate you to reach your goals.
9. Iron sharpens iron. Use whatever drives you to develop the necessary competitive nature to pursue success.

Keep Your Team Close

- When you create a game plan to reach your next level, start with yourself. Be confident in your own mental and physical skills and abilities.
- Your personal team isn't just the players on the field with you; your personal team is any person who has taken a vested interest in your success and that you rely on for guidance and support.
- Take a moment to notice each of your team members: Who is on "your team?" What do you like about them? Those are the characteristics you like about yourself. What do you dislike about your teammates? That is what you dislike about yourself. How do they show support or guidance?
- Every time you step on the field, set the goal to be the best in your position, and play so your team looks good.
- Anyone will cheer for you when you're winning, but it's your team who has your back when you're not hitting your spots.
- Two are better than one because they have a good return on their work; if one falls the other picks him up.
- The Champion leans on his team.
- Find coaches and camps that integrate this kind of motivation and encouragement in their players.

Secret 5
Practice Like It's Game Day

The will to win is the will to prepare to win. Be game-ready every time you step into practice. It's impossible to give 100% every minute, but the Champion gives his best effort all the time, especially at practice.

1. The average player lacks intensity, focus and competitive drive during practice, but will show up on game day wanting to win.
2. The Champion seeks training centered on the right approach in order to improve his skill and advance to his next level.
3. At practice, be self-competitive and self-motivated to perfect game situational strategies and techniques.
4. Practice allows the Champion to think and critique his performance, so during the game he'll be able to relax and react.
5. The athlete who attends camp and listens with full attention to mentors is taking the steps necessary to develop his skills and make himself game ready, so he can consistently raise his Peak Performance.
6. The Champion shows up at practice and game day focused and determined, unwilling to be distracted from his game plan.

Practice Like It's Game Day

- Elevated performance starts at practice.
- Everyone wants to win during the game, only the Champion plays to win at practice.
- In order to achieve success, your game plan must include the habits that you routinely practice.
- The average player may whine and drag his feet during drills that don't interest him, while the Champion accepts every situation as the next challenge on his journey that brings his goals closer.
- Professional baseball champions approach practice with a single-minded focus. They let nothing and no one take them off their game plan.
- Elite athletes practice discipline even down to practicing their breathing.
- They pay attention and make adjustments, so those game-winning plays become instinctive.

Secret 6
Expect Success

The Champion sets his goals, commits himself to those goals, and then pursues those goals with all the ability given to him. To accomplish great things, one must not only plan, but dream, not only act – but believe.

1. The Champion sees and feels the thrill of personal achievement, satisfaction and pride of winning.
2. Visualize the successful completion of every game: every at bat, every play.
3. Every day, visualize the thrill of making the game-changing play in the Championship round!
4. Visualize getting the call from the recruiter, so your concentration and intensity grows.
5. With controlled attention, concentrated energy and sustained effort, you begin to have total confidence in your ability to overcome any obstacle. You will not be denied!
6. Maintain a positive attitude in everything. If you get upset or worried, you are not concentrating.
7. To elevate your game realize you cannot always win, but you *can* always have a winning attitude.
8. Enter every competition without giving mental recognition to the possibility of defeat. You are a winner. Expect to win, this is how you rise.
9. To rise, never quit on the road to success to become stronger and more courageous every day.

Expect Success

- **To be a Champion**, have the courage to take the steps necessary for the success you want and owe yourself.
- Courage is loving the possible. Build your courage muscle at baseball camp.
- Like the Champion, have more courage today than yesterday, and even more courage tomorrow.
- Act like a Champion. Follow your game plan on the path to victory, regardless of obstacles, criticism, circumstances or what others say, think or do.
- Whether you are victorious or not, is not determined in the final score of the game.
- Leave nothing in reserve. Lay it all on the line every time.
- Ultimate success is rooted in your preparation and your ability to execute your skills consistently.
- To be confident in your skill and ability, work with mentors in programs who care about your individual improvement and success.

Secret 7
Remember Where You Started

Track your progress and take nothing for granted. The only way you know if you are progressing through your goals is if you know where you started and know where you're going.

1. Vital to his game plan, the Champion tracks his physical, mental, and emotional progress.
2. Journal your thoughts and feelings around different skills as you work toward mastery.
3. Write down your negative roadblocks and how you feel when you accomplish difficult tasks.
4. The Champion journals something he learns at every practice and after every game.
5. When something "clicks," and the light bulb goes on for you, take a moment to reflect and write about that.
6. The Champion tracks his skill results, speed and accuracy.
7. The Champion sets achievable goals that can be measured to track his improvement.
8. You are a Champion who follows his game plan.
9. Remind yourself of past victories and accomplished goals.

Remember Where You Started

- Be evaluated by an expert like you'll find at The Right Approach Baseball Academy. That way you'll be able to set benchmarks in your game plan and work toward them.
- Keep a journal where you track your progress.

Journal Entry Questions:
- What does my coach say I need to work on?
- What did I do great? Where could I improve? What am I going to do differently next time, so I can improve?
- What obstacles are in my way?
- What changes do I need to make to get beyond those obstacles and stay on my game plan?
- And, how do I feel about this?

- Benchmarks are goals that are achievable and measurable.
- Take nothing for granted.

Secret 8
Find Your *ZONE*

The *Zone* is the place where performance and best effort meet efficiency. The *Zone* is the place you go where you react without having to think.

1. The *Zone* is about clearing your mind of doubt, worry and uncertainty.
2. Remove everything from your mind, so you can simply react to the ball.
3. Watch an MLB relief pitcher walk from the bullpen to the mound. He doesn't look toward the crowd or see who's in the stands. His attention doesn't waiver from the certainty of his pitch-call strategy. He makes it look easy, like playing catch in the school yard.
4. Watch a batter on a hot streak enter the batter's box; he has no stress and no worry about capitalizing on the one pitch left over the plate.
5. This is the zone! When all your practice and preparation arrive at the same time in the same place, culminating in relaxed and seemingly effortless execution of your skills.
6. Know the play you need to make before the ball is in play, and then simply react.
7. You need laser focus, which produces more results than simply the ballplayer's energy by itself.

Find Your *Zone*

- The player who intentionally practices the right approach becomes the instinctive Champion who makes it look effortless.
- The more you play in the zone, the more your stats will rise.
- Working with expert coaches in a camp program will help you to find and develop your zone.
- **How to Find the Zone:** Remember a time when you were in the zone; what did you feel right before? Recreate that feeling.
- Know the play you need to make before the ball is in play.
- Don't second-guess yourself, just react.
- When you're in the zone, notice how your task becomes easy and effortless. Consistency overtakes your concerns.
- You start to feel unstoppable.
- Start to notice when you get out of your head and play in your Zone.

Secret 9
Off the Field and *IN* the Classroom

Your Baseball success is only as good as your current grades. To stay in the game, you've got to make the grade.

1. Scholarships are not given to athletes with poor grades. Earn the title of Student-Athlete.
2. In order to be a Student-Athlete, take the secrets you learn on the field and apply them to your academic studies.
3. When does the Champion give up on the field? *Never!!* Same goes for academics.
4. Your game plan requires you to use the focus and mental toughness you have on the field to rise in your studies.
5. The Champion recognizes his teacher is another coach. Your teacher wants you to succeed in academics that same way your coach wants you to succeed on the field.
6. **Remember Secret 2:** Errors Aren't Failures. Use the lessons from the field to equip your inner Champion in every situation.
7. Classmates are like teammates; form study sessions for subjects, so you can elevate your performance.
8. Use your courses to figure out what you want to continue to study in your future.
9. Eventually you will go "Pro" in something; be the Champion in whatever career you choose.

Off the Field and *IN* the Classroom

- Excellence in all things matter to the Champion.
- D grades don't cut it; notice who in your class is achieving the grade you want and ask for help.
- Put in the extra individual effort on the field and in the classroom to experience success.
- Keep accountable to your teachers. Each week ask your teachers for a status update: current grade, plus areas for improvement.
- Turn assignments in on time and completed to a standard of excellence.
- It is impossible to be a stupid Champion. But, if you coast on your talent instead of applying yourself, you may live to regret it.
- Remember your game plan requires you to plan for your future and that includes a college education in a field of study that interests you and motivates you to live your dreams.

Secret 10
Regret Nothing

Be alert and be active. Be looking for and be prepared for your chance. When you have the chance to try out for the next level, rise to the challenge. Find a way to take advantage of every opportunity, or the chance to live your dream may just pass you by. If you don't take the opportunity, you will always wonder, "What if…?"

1. You'll never know what you're truly capable of, if you don't take the risk with your whole heart.
2. The Champion turns his fear into excitement, and it fuels his competitive nature.
3. What sets the Champion apart is, he doesn't let anything get in the way of reaching his peak performance and his goal.
4. When the Champion looks back on his life, he can be proud of the opportunities that he pursued and the risks he took.
5. The Champion leaves nothing in reserve; he leaves his all on the field, in the classroom, in the boardroom, and in his life.
6. If things didn't work out, it was never because the Champion didn't give his best effort.
7. Being a Champion is as much about *who you are,* as what you do.

Regret Nothing

- The worst thing for any one of us is to look back and say, "I should've or could've…"
- Recognize you're always playing for the MLB and other professional organizations.
- At any moment, someone may be looking at you for your chance to raise your level of play.

Avoid Knucklehead Syndrome:

- Even players with skill and talent risk becoming knuckleheads by drinking, partying, using drugs or making other poor choices.
- Knuckleheads lack discipline and concentration.
- Knuckleheads think they can coast on their talent, but you can't just coast.
- Don't doubt for a second, that the guy who misses his chance doesn't live to regret it.
- This is not your game plan. Fully pursue your dream. Choose dedication, discipline and determination.
- After making some knuckleheaded choices, one guy was able to turn it around. With renewed dedication and discipline, he redoubled his efforts and went from MiLB A to MLB in just one season.

- Find a mentor who supports your game plan.
- Have the courage to make choices and take risks necessary for the success you want and deserve.

Secret 11
Million Dollar Asset

Your body is your first million dollar asset. Taking care of your entire body is the key to your game plan. Your body needs to be in optimal condition if you plan to have a long career. There comes a moment in every Champion's life when you realize that bigger, better, stronger just is not enough to rise. Play smarter, right now.

1. To edge out his competition, the Champion needs a program that emphasizes healthy function, as well as strategy, power, endurance and skill.
2. The Champion follows a game plan that supports peak performance without compromising his body, so he can pursue a long career.
3. Many of us have been conditioned to associate pain with physical improvement; and we're taught the more it hurts, the more you get out of it.
4. Don't be fooled. Learn to pay attention to your body. *Pain is an indication that something is wrong.* A top coaching staff will focus on health as much as performance.
5. We are all different in strength, endurance, flexibility and temperament. Your program needs to consider your specific needs.
6. If your game plan includes what you learn about your body's needs, you'll start to build your foundation of healthy function that will last your career and your lifetime.

Million Dollar Asset

- A solid game plan doesn't just include strength and skill training. The plan for improving performance includes: what you feed your body, mental toughness, and decreasing the chance of injury.
- You only get one body, so take care of it.
- Many micro-tears, like strain or sprain, can progress into major injuries when you don't take care of yourself properly.
- These micro-tears, when ignored, kill your career. Just take a look at the DLs –disabled lists.
- When you gear up for an event, you put your body into a state of stress. Stress can compromise performance.
- Decrease your chance of injury by following a repair and recovery post-performance game plan.
- Your competitive edge prepares your body and mind to perform, as well as to recover after competition.
- When you play for a coach, you are trusting them with your money-maker; not all coaches deserve that trust.
- Don't play for coaches who overuse your body. Instead, play for coaches who allow you time to rest and recover between competitions and who have earned your trust.

Secret 12
Align Your Mind

Confidence on the field starts with mental toughness. The Champion knows his body will follow his thoughts.

1. You are what you think. Your body is like a robot just following every thought you think.
2. Heart and mind have to agree with what you pursue in order to get your best results.
3. Your unconscious (body) and conscious (mind) must be in agreement for you to unleash your ultimate success.
4. The Champion knows that to maintain his rank and reach his Next Level, the difference that makes the difference is limiting his Mental Errors.
5. Skill and talent aren't enough without mental sharpness: the ability to think strategically and quickly is stressed at camps that are next level-focused.
6. Players who get "caught sleeping" allow the Champion to make the play that costs them the game.
7. The Champion knows to set goals and work backward through achievable results.
8. Include goals for every milestone that you'll need to achieve in order to know you're on the path to reaching your success.

Align Your Mind

- If you think you can't, then you won't.
- The difference that makes the difference is your ability to change your perspective.
- Errors aren't failures, but what you tell yourself fuels your performance, and negativity can cost you your dreams.
- When you force yourself to execute a skill, you tighten up, hindering your ability to perform.
- Better to relax and breathe.
- Your dream is to play professional baseball, but that's a dream, not a goal.
- The coaches at TRA baseball academy teach their athletes to set SMART goals. (Specific, Measurable, Achievable, Realistic and Timed)
- Your game plan must include: benchmarks, milestones, and SMART goals.

Secret 13
Nutrition: Junk In, Junk *OUT*

NO amount of hard work can make up for a lack of proper food, rest and hydration. Successful performance starts with the right nutrition and hydration as the foundation to your game plan.

1. Your body gets important nutrients for maintaining health and supporting your athletic performance from eating the right foods.
2. Food either fuels your body or drains your energy.
3. Simple Carbohydrates (soda, sports drinks, sugar, etc.) may initially spike your energy, but will ultimately crash your energy and endurance.
4. Complex carbohydrates activate muscle activity, endurance and energy.
5. Your body burns complex carbohydrates during hard exercise, which provides fuel for your body's performance.
6. Protein is essential for building and repairing muscles, red blood cells, soft tissue, etc.
7. Protein from food is broken into amino acids, which are the building blocks of muscle protein.
8. Your body needs healthy fat, but too much body fat is not healthy for solid athletic performance.
9. Vitamins and minerals are obtained from food and are essential for Peak Performance.
10. Dehydrated muscles become stiff and weak. And they are more likely to be injured.

Nutrition: Junk In, Junk *OUT*

- Most athletes are slightly dehydrated during performance and don't even know it.
- Drinking water before warm-up as part of your nutritional game plan, increases hydration and decreases fatigue and muscle weakness.
- Water stabilizes your body temperature, cooling your body during exercise.
- Water carries nutrients to your cells and lubricates your joints.
- The first sign of dehydration is fatigue, then cramping.
- Complex carbohydrates are found in fiber, 100% whole grains, and colored vegetables.
- Simple Carbohydrates from soda, sports drinks and sugar can spike then crash your energy during competition.
- Protein alone doesn't build muscles.
- Protein provides the ingredients for the body to use during exercise in order to build muscle and increase strength.
- Elevate your performance by preparing your body with nutritional fuel.

Secret 14
Competitive Edge

Only a fool competes without recognizing that the Competitive Edge is how you prepare for – and recover from – competition. Learn to integrate your competitive edge as you train with TRA coaching staff.

1. The right approach to Peak Performance includes quality rest and recovery to avoid the risk of repetitive strain and micro-injuries.
2. Commit to a pre-event program that involves warm-up, stretching, rotational movements and conditioning, so his muscles know it's time to get to work, right now.
3. Even 8 minutes of a pre-event stretch routine prepares your body and mind for competition.
4. Having a pre-event game plan decreases injury potential, reduces muscle tension and anxiety, and improves mental clarity and focus.
5. Stretch to recover from muscle fatigue, decreasing soreness, and repairing muscle.
6. Post-event cool down is a scaled down version of skills and pre-event stretches.
7. After activity, 10 minutes of massage can decrease stress and inflammation, and increase immunity and energy.

Competitive Edge

- A strong, <u>flexible</u>, <u>pre-stretched</u> muscle, resists stress better that a strong, <u>stiff</u>, <u>un-stretched</u> muscle.
- As we age, we lose hydration and our muscles stiffen, making it harder to bounce back from physical activity.
- Go for quality repetitions over quantity.
- Stretching routinely improves your body's longevity.
- Warm-up using movements related to skill performance.
- Warm up to throw. Don't throw to warm up.
- When sick, the Champion may not go full-out physically, but can still give a best effort and practice mentally.
- Failing to prepare is preparation for failure But, the will to win is the will to prepare to win.
- The edge in competition is all in your preparation.

Secret 15
Elevate Your Game

As you rise to the Next Level, everyone has talent and skill. What separates them, from the ones who reach their dreams, is they have mastered the right approach.

1. Embrace what makes you unique. What others see as a disability may just be the obstacle you need to overcome to reach your goals, and live your dream.
2. The Champion's game plan focuses on the details.
3. The Champion is dedicated to his goal. Be dedicated to your game plan and your goals.
4. In high school, everyone strives to be an All-American. At the professional level, everyone strives for greatness. Strive for greatness, not the award.
5. The Champion is the average of the 5 people he spends the most time around. Surround yourself with mentors who are who you want to be.
6. The Champion's greatest asset is his power to choose. Decide to be a positive influence.
7. Your biggest competition isn't another player playing your position. Your biggest competition is yourself.
8. Find what drives you, and use whatever it takes to motivate you to rise in excellence.

Elevate Your Game

- It's not how you start; it's how you finish.
- If the journey to reach your dream was easy, everybody would do it.
- Execute routine plays consistently.
- Be ready and alert to make the unexpected play.
- Know your strengths and weaknesses. Play into your strengths and minimize your weaknesses.
- Limit your errors, increase your opportunities.
- Be proud of your accomplishments.
- Do not ever give up on yourself.
- A masterpiece isn't perfect; if you examine it closely, you see the flaws and mistakes, but when you step back and take in the whole, the errors blend with execution to create masterful moments.
- You are a masterpiece.
- Find mentors and programs that will help you cultivate consistent discipline, dedication and determination.
- In a race, everyone runs, but only one gets the prize. Run your race to win.

Don't let this be the end. Let it be the beginning...

Now is the time to invest in yourself. Sign up for camp. Rise to your next level. For the most current schedule for lessons, clinics and camps, go to:

www.TRABaseball.com

And...

Tweet/share that you finished this book.

Please star rate this book.

Reviews are solid gold to writers. Please take a few minutes to give us some itty bitty feedback.

ABOUT THE AUTHORS

Curt is the founder of The Right Approach (TRA) Baseball Academy. He is a certified pitching coach. Playing and coaching for over 30 years, he has coached elite athletes with current and former professional players. This has allowed him to learn the secrets needed to rise to ultimate success – knowledge he could have used as a youngster. With his experience, Curt works to help the next generation of Baseball players to rise. Seeing successes and shortcomings on a daily basis allows his team of experts to pinpoint how a young player can maximize his talent and live his dreams. TRA combines the physical with the mental aspects of playing Baseball to help develop the complete player, thus preparing for Baseball success.

www.TRABaseball.com

With over 15 years of coaching and mentoring experience (beginner-college), Amy left teaching to open Serenity Jean because she saw the need to bridge the gap between physical stress and quality of life. She is a holistic health practitioner and certified massage therapist. She is a licensed skin expert, Master Hypnotherapist and Master NLP practitioner. She's been featured in the Inland Empire Magazine, has guest-lectured for PossAbilities Women's Cycle Clinic and works with professional and amateur athletes, so they can gain the competitive edge and live their dream.

www.SerenityJean.com

**If you enjoyed this Itty Bitty® Book,
you might also enjoy…**

- **Your Amazing Itty Bitty® Communicating With Your Teenager Book** – Chris Alisa

- **Your Amazing Itty Bitty® Family Leadership Book** – Jacqueline T. D. Huynh

- **Your Amazing Itty Bitty® Parenting Teens Book** – Gretchen Downey

With many more Amazing Itty Bitty® Books to available on line…

www.ingramcontent.com/pod-product-compliance
Lightning Source LLC
Chambersburg PA
CBHW061304040426
42444CB00010B/2507